GOD NEVER LEFT ME

GOD NEVER LEFT ME

JAANNA JAY

Contents

Introduction

This is a true story of how God woke me up and set me free.

CHAPTER 1

My Childhood

I was born in London in 1972. Mum had nine children in total, four previous children before meeting my dad. He had two before meeting my mum, then they had five together. As a young child growing up, I always heard Mum singing about Jesus on a Sunday morning whilst cooking the rice and peas for dinner. We were so spoilt that she would cook Jamaican food for my dad and something else for us because at that age we did not appreciation good food.

Mum was a quiet, gentle woman with no friends. That's a lie. She had one friend called Bee-Bee from Trinidad and Tobago; a cute little Indian-looking woman who always made us laugh with her accent. I swear she spoke at 100 miles per hour; she was a little bullet. Mum was a stay-at-home mum because my brother who was born directly after me had special needs.

She had so many stories to tell us about her growing up in Jamaica and how her mischievous brother got licked down by a duppy! He was her favourite brother though, the one she followed to England.

My dad was from Portland in Jamacia. He had jet black Indian-looking hair, and the ladies loved him. He could and would talk with anyone. Dad worked for British Telecom. He would leave the house at 5:30 every morning and come back at 6 every evening. Every Thursday was pocket money day, and he would bring us all the chocolate we could eat. Dad spoilt us but he was really jealous over Mum and would argue with her constantly. The only time you would hear my mum nag him was when he would light up his Benson & Hedges cigarette in the bathroom. Mum didn't like the smoke and plus she had asthma.

My parents rented a room in Mum's friend's house until the local council gave us our own four-bedroom flat. It was a bit cramped with all of us living under one roof but coming from one bedroom, it was heaven. I remember way back in the early eighties, a man called Brother Daley moved into the flat upstairs and started talking to Mum about church.

'Me likkle son is autistic and he is hard work, so I can't come but the pickney dem can go to sometime.'

My dad was totally against it and argued with my mum about it. His church was the betting office. He loved to bet on the horses and the dogs, anything that moved really.

Brother Daley was very persistent and one evening, out of the blue, me and my three older sisters were being loaded into his blue van with windows that slid open from side to side. After what seemed like hours and hours, we arrived at a house.

'I don't like this house. It's big and cold and who are all these people?' I was around eight years old and this was the last place I wanted to be.

Brother Daley helped to put out the wooden chairs in the front room and then an adult put us all on separate seats. They started to pray and talked in this strange language. They started to talk about Jesus and I thought, *Oh, I know him. My mum sings about him on Sunday when she's cooking the rice and peas.*

I started to pay attention to hear what they knew about Jesus because all Mum ever sung was, 'Some sweet day, when life is over. Some sweet day, praise the Lord, I'm going away.' Where was she gong to and were kids allowed to go too? I wanted to know more about this man called Jesus. They stood up one by one and started talking about all the things Jesus had done for them and all I could remember thinking was, *Wow! Jesus is kind. I wanna meet him.*

I listened with pricked ears and began to feel a rushing in my heart and belly and then, for some reason, I started to cry.

'This little girl needs to be baptised,' said the woman sitting beside me with the flying saucer hat on.

She began hugging me and after a little while, I stopped crying. After what seemed like hours and hours, the prayer meeting was over and we all went home. My older sister told my mum we couldn't go back because I had started crying for no reason. Mum agreed we didn't have to go back, which my dad was happy about. Brother Daley tried to persuade my mum to let us go a few more times but I think it was easier for my mum that we didn't just so my dad wouldn't argue with her.

We got older and the flat became more and more cramped. My dad started to argue with my mum about my older siblings and them getting a job and moving out even though they had barely just left school. He argued day in day out until they moved out one by one.

In August 1988 we moved into a house in South London. I was fifteen nearly sixteen but I was already working as part of a youth training scheme and earning money. My dad was still arguing with my mum day and night about events that happened years ago, before I was born! I couldn't take anymore. Three weeks after moving into the new house, I told Mum I was leaving home.

'What yuh mean leaving home? Where are you going?'

'I'm moving in with Helen. She's got a three-bedroom flat and said that I could stay with her.'

Mum gave me the look but I left with all my clothes in a small plastic bag.

By the age of eighteen, I had a boyfriend that I moved in with. By 1995 I found myself single and living in a hostel. All I had to do was stay there for six months and I would get a place of my own.

CHAPTER 2

Girl, He Is Not My Type

Marcia was someone me and my sister Kerry met at the same time. She quickly became a good friend of the whole family. Her family lived a few hundred miles away in the country so she quickly became a part of ours.

Marcia had fallen for a guy called Buks who often went to the pub just down the street from her house and being the good friends we were, we went with her just so she could see him.

That was where it all started: Marcia having a crush on Buks. Buks was of mixed-race heritage with a big forehead hence the name.

January 1996 saw them trying to hook me up with his so-called cousin.

That weekend, as usual, we went to the pub. It was kind of boring to me but I had nothing else to do, so

I tagged along as usual. Marcia was thick in body and all the men loved her. My sister Kerry had a good shape with straight long coolie hair. Me, I was straight up and down like an ironing board with slightly thicker hair. I didn't get much attention from men. Not the nice ones anyway.

One night, Buks brought his cousin with him who was fresh from yard (Jamaica).

Marcia came running over to me where I was sat at the bar with a big grin on her face to tell me his cousin liked me.

I took one look and said, 'Hell to the no.'

He looked about ten years old, was about five feet ten inches with a nice dark brown complexion and tight coils. He was very skinny back then. Anyway, I didn't want no yardie because all they wanted was their stay in England. No thank you!

As I began to screw up my face at the sheer thought of it, he started to head in my direction. I turned around to Marcia to see she had walked off fast in the opposite direction.

What the hell was she doing? Didn't I just tell her I wasn't interested? To make things worse, I couldn't even get up and leave because the pub was packed with men and I was not about to walk past them all congregating by the exit.

He introduced himself as Lindon, Buks' cousin.

I said hi without even looking at him.

He began to talk and talk and talk. It was a one-sided conversation with me nodding and saying yeah a couple of times until he mentioned Jamaica.

My eyes lit up. I absolutely loved Jamaica and I had only just come back a few months before. We spoke about Jamaica for about three hours and by the end of the evening, I actually thought he was quite pleasant.

For the next three weekends we went to the pub and, as usual, Buks was there with his cousin Lindon who we now found out wasn't his cousin at all.

'So, how come you know Buks then if you're not related?'

He said he was sleeping on Buks' mum's sofa because he had nowhere to live. His aunt, who he used to live with, died six months after he arrived in the UK.

I asked him why he didn't just go back home to Jamaica.

He said he always dreamt of living in England and wanted to make a better life for himself and that's why he wrote to his aunt to ask if he could stay with her until he got on his feet. But she died and her husband was now the only one living in the house. He was adamant he wasn't going back there because his aunt's husband took a particular liking to young men.

'How can he be gay and he was married to your aunt?'

Lindon explained that his aunt knew about his preference but they were old school and believed that once you were married, you were married for life. Besides, they didn't have any children so they basically lived separate lives in the same house.

Weeks passed and me and Lindon spoke more and more when we saw each other at the pub.

The next weekend came and Marcia decided to have a break from the pub so we decided to stayed at her flat for the evening even though she spent most of it on the phone to Buks. At around 2 a.m. there was a loud bang on the front door. We looked at each other and I told her not to open the door but she got all excited and giggly thinking that it could be Buks.

We peeped behind the curtain of the kitchen window to see Lindon standing there.

'What on earth is he doing here?'

Before I could finish my sentence, Marcia had opened the door and let him in, then had the cheek to say she was tired and going to bed !

I was pissed to say the least It was 2 in the morning and all I wanted was to go to sleep.

Lindon talked for hours about everything and nothing. I was upset but too well-mannered to tell him to go home. I kinda got the feeling he didn't want to go back to Buks' mum's house that night. He told me that Buks' mum didn't want him on her sofa anymore and he had to move out.

I asked him how he was eating and who gave him money.

He lifted up his top lip and showed me little pieces of silver foil under his high cheekbones.

'Oh my gosh, is that drugs? What are you doing Lindon? You do know if the police catch you, they'll deport you and you'll never be able to come back to the UK.'

He told me it was crack and he was shotting. He had no other way of making money. I was horrified. Of course, I had heard of cocaine but never actually seen it and I couldn't believe he had all that wrapped in foil and stacked under his cheekbones.

'You gotta get rid of it. This is not right.' I mean I know I had smoked weed in the past but his cocaine thing. Nah, I wasn't getting mixed up in anything like that.

I soon found myself feeling really sorry for him because all he wanted was a chance of having a better life and I began to put myself in his position. He also told me about Buks' mum and I wasn't going to lie, my heart hurt for him.

One thing led to another and soon we were an item, and immediately stopped selling drugs.

CHAPTER 3

Moving in Day

At last, my flat was ready to move in to. It was all mine and I loved it. There was no one to tell me anything. I could do anything I wanted. This was my first flat since leaving home all those years ago. Lindon was still living at Buks' mum's house but came round almost every day after work. Things were going really well. I got another job earning a bit more money and was really happy.

Around two months after moving in, my doorbell rang and I knew it was Lindon because he always came around the same time every evening after work. I went downstairs to open the door, but before I could even say hi, he walked past me and up the stairs with the tatty brown suitcase that he had brought from Jamaica in his hand.

'Umm, excuse me, where are you going with that?'

He kept walking right on past me and up the stairs mumbling something about not being able to stay at Buks' mum's house anymore.

I was in disbelief. Did he just walk past me and put his suitcase in my cupboard? What does he think he's doing?

Without even looking at me, he said he didn't have anywhere else to go and stretched himself out my bed turning his back towards me. Maybe, no not maybe, I *was* a pushover because instead of telling him that he couldn't stay, I thought of how his aunt had died and how he had no one else in England that he could turn to. I told myself I couldn't be as wicked as to let him sleep on the streets. I decided that I would let him stay a few days. After all, he was working on a building site so he wouldn't be living off me, would he? Even though he still had to pay to go to the fake college so he could get his passport stamped so the Government wouldn't deport him.

Six months went by and I began to feel really sick and went to the doctors. The doctor asked if I had missed a period.

'Oh no, I'm not pregnant. I have funny periods and it's normal for me to miss three or even four months.'

The doctor said she would send me to the early pregnancy unit because of the pain in my abdomen.

Was this doctor even listening to me? I had a period last month. I mean, it was a light one but it was still a period.

Reluctantly, I went to the early pregnancy unit the next morning. I laid on the couch and the doctor said if I was pregnant I'd see a tiny dot. I let out a little chuckle. Me... pregnant? Ha ha ha.

The doctor put the cold clear gel on my stomach and began moving it around and around and around. What was she looking for? Surely she could see there was nothing there by now. I glanced over at the monitor to see the sonographer was actually taking measurements. I nearly fell off the bed in shock. I could see the outline of a baby kicking its legs and sucking its thumb.

After about five minutes, the sonographer turned to me with my mouth hanging open with shock. She said according to her measurements I was around six months pregnant. The sonographer didn't realise I had not even done a pregnancy test at this point. That was December 1996 and my due date was March 1997.

I walked all the way home in a daze. Me pregnant!. I told Lindon as soon as he came home from work and, of course, he was happy. I mean, who wouldn't be? That was his UK passport. Oops, silly me, of course I meant his first child.

CHAPTER 4

The Proposal

Christmas Day 1996 and me and Lindon were having our first Christmas together. I made a roast chicken with all the trimmings. It was perfect. After dinner I washed up the plates with my big belly then went to the front room to watch a bit of TV to see Lindon kneeling down on one knee. I remember seeing him open a box and hearing the words: will you marry me? This was unexpected to say the least, so to say I was in shock was an understatement. I never expected this. I began to remember that as a small child from around the age of around seven, I constantly dreamt about being married and standing in front of a house with my husband. It was the same dream in the same house time after time…

I snapped out of the place I had drifted off to and thought, *He's only doing this so he can stay in*

England. Why would he want to get married? He's only twenty-one and I'm only twenty-three. I thought long and hard about it and even though I was pregnant by him I wasn't sure I loved him enough to marry him.

The next day I decided to myself that I would marry him but only to help him get his stay in the UK because even though he didn't say it, I knew this was the reason. He couldn't love me that much to want to spend the rest of his life with me in such a short space of time. He is lucky that I've got such a soft heart. If his aunt hadn't died I doubt if he would be here right now.

Time seemed to fly really quickly and Lindon began to get regular work with an older guy called Gregory who he knew from Jamaica. I began to prepare for our first child: a boy called Terry born in March 1997.

Two months later without telling any of my family me and Lindon got married in a registry office still keeping in the back of my mind that I was only doing it to help him, which is something I never ever spoke out verbally to him or anyone else.

A year went by and our love began to grow. Lindon was still working and giving me what he could for food, sending some money to his parents and trying to sort out his stay with the Home Office. It felt as though I was always just about managing to survive with all the bills and trying to provide for Terry and it also became evident to me that Lindon, for some reason, became jealous of his son. I told myself that this is how Jamaican men are and that he is still young and would change. All I had to do was give him some time and he would be ok.

Man, I found so many excuses why he had very little time for his son.

One Sunday morning out of the blue immigration decided to pay us an unannounced visit. I ran into the bedroom to get myself decent. They checked all over the flat even in the bathroom. Terry was scared and began to cry. He scooted over to his dad to be picked up while I was in the bedroom still trying to get myself together.

'Well,' the immigration officer said, 'It's obvious to us that you live here and the fact that the baby has gone straight over to you shows that he knows you. We are satisfied and won't be back again.'

No less than two weeks later Lindon got his passport back with his indefinite leave to remain in the UK. Lindon was shocked but elated and so was I. We had often heard stories of people waiting for years just for a two-year extension and here he was with his leave to remain. I remember thanking God because that was such a financial burden and we no longer had to think about. Life was about to get better, or so I thought.

CHAPTER 5

The Betrayal

As usual, 8 a.m. on the dot, Gregory was outside beeping his car horn for Lindon and, as usual, Lindon was late.

I asked him what area he was working in so I would know roughly what time to start dinner.

Before running out the door he said he was working in Gregory's wife house because she needed things fixing.

'Okay, see you later,' I said.

I cooked dinner to make sure Lindon had food to eat after a hard day's work which is something I did every day. But 6 p.m. came and went.

That's funny, I thought, *Lindon is never late home. I wonder if he's okay.*

I called him five times that evening and each time his phone went to voicemail. I was really worried and thought something must have happened. He had never been late home and he always answered his phone. I must have called Lindon at least fifteen times between 6 p.m. and 11 p.m. My head had a million thoughts going round it. What if he had been in a fight and injured or what if Gregory had crashed his van and they were lying injured somewhere? My mind was racing in all different directions. All but one.

I went into our bedroom and began to dig up old papers and then looked in Lindon's old diary he had brought from Jamaica with all the important phone numbers in it. Bingo! I found Gregory's mobile number. He would know where Lindon was. I called the number and it began to ring.

Gregory finally answered after what seemed like five minutes and I asked him if he knew where Lindon was. Now Gregory was over fifty years old but he was acting as shady as hell. Couldn't he hear the panic in my voice? He told me he knew where he was, but he couldn't tell me. I would have to wait for Lindon to call me. Did this man know who I was? Did he know that I wasn't the side piece, I was his wife.

'You were at my bloody wedding, Gregory. Why are you acting like this?'

I was mad. Really mad. I was worried about where my husband was and Gregory was giving nothing away. It was 11 p.m. for heaven's sake.

I began to pace up and down. I was no longer just worried, I was angry as well.

I manged to somehow fall asleep and when I eventually woke up the bedroom light was still on from the night before. I listened with my eyes wide open without even breathing to see if I could hear Lindon walking around in the flat. It was dead quiet. There was no one here. Lindon still hadn't come back. I checked my phone. No missed calls, no voicemail and no text messages. I checked the bathroom to see if he had come home, showered and gone back to work without wanting to wake me but the bath was dry. He hadn't come home.

I began to get myself and the baby ready to go out for the day then heard the key turn in the front door. I had a sense of relief and anger all at the same time. I checked the time on my phone. It was 11.20 a.m.

Lindon walked up the stairs right past me into the bedroom wearing a strange white boiler suit thing.

'Where have you been Lindon and what have you got on, where are your clothes?'

Without looking at me, he said he couldn't answer any questions right now. He said he was tired and needed to sleep. He went into our bedroom and shut the door. I felt confused, so confused. This man that I was so worried about all night, pacing all over the bedroom floor for had no time to explain where he had been.

Now you have to understand that my whole family, apart from my dad, was quiet and reserved. We didn't argue, cuss or fight and unless you lived close by us, you didn't hear or see us. To be totally honest, I didn't know how to deal with this except to be quiet which was what I saw my mum do every time my dad started to cuss. I had never heard my mother swear a day in her life and I didn't either. It just wasn't my thing.

I grabbed up my baby and I stormed out of the house. Boy, was I mad.

I stayed out for most of the day and returned home later that evening after calming down and was determined to find out exactly what was going on.

As I turned my key in the front door, I could hear him laughing and joking with his mum on the phone who lived in Jamaica.

I put the baby down and watched him spread out with his legs across the arm of the chair swinging them like a big idiot. I walked past him a few times giving him eye contact to let him see that I was pissed. He didn't get the message and he didn't get off the phone.

Then I heard him say to his mum, 'Maybe I didn't do it right. That's why she said I raped her.'

What? Did I just hear right? Did he say rape?

His mum replied with, 'You will be okay, son. Don't worry.'

Hold on a minute, was someone joking? Was this a prank? Did I just hear what I thought I heard? My husband, left out for work this morning, has somehow ended up having sex with someone and being accused of rape and his Christian mum was consoling him. I felt as though I had been run over by a ten-ton lorry. I couldn't breathe and my chest began to tighten up. This has got to be a joke, this is not real and I'm gonna wake up any minute now.

Around ten minutes later, he came off the phone. I asked him what was going on. He replied, with a big smirk on his face, that Gregory's step-daughter had accused him of rape.

'What do you mean rape? How?'

I had to pump Lindon for answers as though it was none of my business and I had no right to question him.

He said he was stripping the wallpaper in her bedroom. She took off her knickers and said he could have it if she could wear the thick gold chain he had around his neck. He told me that he had sex with her but he ejaculated after a few seconds because she was big.

Huh? was that supposed to make me feel better with that extra added detail?

He said that when he had finished, she asked for his chain but he told her no because I would notice it was missing from around his neck. After having sex with her, he went to get some lunch from the local takeaway and by the time he got back, the police were there waiting for him blue lights and all!

'You dirty stinking piece of crap! How could you do this to us, Lindon?'

Deep down inside I knew he didn't rape her. He was just too laid back to do anything like that but I didn't care. Did he even give me a second thought when he unzipped his trousers? And to make matters worse, he was making a joke of it on the phone with his mum and the woman didn't even tell him to try to console me. She never once asked how I was feeling which didn't surprise me really. Although she knew I was his wife and he was living under my roof, all she ever said was 'say hi to your wife' at the end of every conversation. To say that I was broken was an understatement. I felt as though my whole life had just fallen apart.

I felt humiliated and told Lindon he had to leave that night. I felt physically sick and needed some space. I looked at our gorgeous son and thought, *How could he do this to us?*

Lindon packed his brown suitcase and left. He didn't go very far; his late aunt's house was only five minutes around the corner and he still had the key. Lucky for Lindon, his aunt's husband had died a month before so it was empty.

After two weeks Lindon decided he missed his son and wanted to see him, so I said we would arrange a time, but almost immediately he began coming round at 10 p.m. stating that he was working so he couldn't come round to see Terry any earlier. Then he'd fall asleep on the living room couch. I hated the sight of him. I felt like being sick every time I saw him. How could I have been so stupid? Why did I ever marry a Jamaican?

CHAPTER 6

Baby Number Two

When Terry was about three, I moved into a two-bedroom place. It was really nice and I was happy again. Lindon and I were still separated with him coming over regularly to see Terry.

He pressured me all the time about us getting back together. He said he was fixing up his late aunt's house to sell it and that he had contacted a solicitor to get the ball rolling. He told me about this great life he wanted to give us. When he saw I couldn't be bought, he started to accuse me of being a wicked and nasty person for leaving him to starve in his dead aunt's empty flat and that all I wanted was another man. He put a whole lot of pressure and guilt on me and called me stupid, but I let him move back in with us.

Although Lindon was still working, money was tight because he had started to pay the solicitors and fixing up his aunt's place with the money he earned. As usual, I held it down paying all the bills and providing the food. Then while on the pill, you guessed it, I became pregnant with baby number two.

It was a girl. Can you believe it, one of each: a girl and a boy!

We were like a proper family. Life was getting better.

One afternoon, I turned on the TV and could not believe what I was seeing. Two aeroplanes had just crashed into the World Trade Center.

I looked up to the sky and said, 'God, this world is too evil. I can't do this without you, Lord.'

Right there and then I decided I was going to go to church. I told Lindon I was going to go to our local church and he was cool with the idea, he even came with me.

My family felt complete. We were both working and trying to live right. Lindon's aunt's house sold. Unfortunately, her husband's family got the bulk of the money because he was the last one to die. Besides, Lindon didn't really know his aunt until he arrived in London so it wasn't like he was being robbed of anything but, of course, that wasn't the way he saw it.

We continued going to church and Lindon got baptised. Wow, I never saw that coming! He quickly became an officer and an usher in the church and painted the inside of the church from top to bottom. Everyone loved him and sung his praises all the time, He began doing work in most of the church brothers' and sisters' homes. There was nothing he could not do; he only had to be shown how to do something once and he could do it.

Lindon was still upset on the sale of his aunt's house because out of £265,000 the house sold for, he only received £40,000, which he said he was going to buy a house with. Lindon had also got a real job working as a handyman for the local council. He was earning a decent wage and I was working for the bank. Call me paranoid but his behaviour began to change and I sensed a shift.

In 2003 we began to view houses. We couldn't afford much because house prices were on their way up. Lindon told me that he may not put my name on the house. This was not something I had even thought about, but obviously he had. What a damn cheek coming from the man who moved himself into my flat without asking , I put it to the back of my mind and didn't give it another thought.

Lindon and I had been married for six years. We were going from a two-bedroom flat with two children to now buying a house. Life was perfect. Both Terry and Tasha were in school and I was back to working full time again.

We eventually found a nice three-bedroom terraced house and Lindon sorted out the mortgage. This was something he forgot to mention to me. Three went by and Lindon mentioned that he wasn't earning enough money by himself and had been advised that, unless he put my name down on the mortgage, he wouldn't be able to get it, he was not happy!. God works in mysterious ways, I was cracking up with laugher inside.

'No problem,' I said and signed the mortgage agreement. That was the first and only time I ever laid eyes on it.

We had to rent it out to the local council for two years because it was a buy-to-let. I didn't see a penny of the money he collected while renting out the house and I didn't ask. Then after two years, we evicted the tenants and were finally able to move in.

CHAPTER 7

We Bought a House

Moving day was hectic. I had the two kids with me moving the smaller items to the new house in my car. I had to make about five trips back and forth and was knackered. Lindon used his work van to move the white goods such as the washing machine and fridge freezer. I was so excited I began to arrange the furniture in the new place and almost immediately Lindon became very snappy. He didn't want the bed where I had put it in and other little things which wouldn't have been a problem before. I hung a picture on the wall and he told me, in no uncertain terms, he didn't want the picture on the wall.

I began to feel as though I was in the way. Nothing I did concerning the house was the way he wanted it. I put it down to the stress of moving and brushed it off. We agreed that Lindon would pay for the mortgage and the council tax and I would pay for all the other bills including buying all the kids' clothes and paying for school dinners. He never gave me money for any of the kids.

Lindon worked all day, just like I did, and when he came home he decorated the house. It was really nice. He was definitely a master in everything he did and he soon turned the three bedrooms into four bedrooms, two bathrooms. He got a lot of the material free from work. He chose everything from the bath to the tiles even the kitchen. He didn't tell me or ask my opinion about anything and when I gave my suggestions, the answer was always no. I started to feel like an unwelcomed visitor in my own home and the children were being watched everywhere they went in the house to make sure they were not destroying it.

Was Lindon okay? He knew the children were brought up properly and wouldn't destroy anything. Besides, they were too scared of him to touch his things anyway. What was he on? Jheez!

Lindon finally got his British citizenship and didn't even tell me. I overheard him telling his mum on the phone. I sensed an even bigger shift and, all of a sudden, my opinion on anything at all didn't matter.

By now I was deeply regretting moving out of my council flat. The fact that we lived in this beautiful house with a big garden didn't matter A lot of people who knew us saw the change in him said I was stupid for giving my flat up, but I knew it was illegal for me to sub-let and I didn't want to do anything that would cause me to get a criminal record. After all, I was now a baptised Christian and tried to live as upright as possible.

The years went by and I began to shrink inside. I just got on with life on auto-pilot, you could say. I brought the kids to school every day, went to work, came home, cooked dinner, bathed the kids and sorted their clothes for the next day while all he did was work on his precious house. He had little to no time for the kids although he would take them to the park once in a blue moon.

All of a sudden, he had exalted himself above everyone in the house and even above most of the people in the church we attended, although on a Sunday he looked like a devoted husband and father. The church members continued to sing his praises because he would run to help them fix their houses at the drop of a hat. Even I was invisible to them. So, how was it possible I'm pregnant again?

CHAPTER 8

Here We Go Again…
Baby Number Three

By 2006 we had been married for nine years. Quite honestly, I don't even know how we made it that far. At that point Lindon spoke to me out of duty and nothing else. He said that he was this great officer of the church and so anointed and the whole church would soon see when he was rich and had his many mansions. He knew most of the Bible off by heart and could quote any chapter and verse where as I was the total opposite.

I told Lindon I was pregnant again and he reckoned God had told him already because, according to him, God told him everything. At least that was what he told the kids so he could control them. I, of course, told them that was rubbish and they shouldn't be scared of him. He was hardly ever nice to me or the kids and tried to control them with fear. Lindon accused the kids of doing all sorts of things to his house. I remember one cold winter a bird had flown directly into the window of the loft extension and he accused them of breaking it until he found the bird dead on the floor. Then another time he accused them of drawing on the wall. My daughter Tasha was only five at the time but said it was her so her older brother Terry wouldn't get beaten for it. Terry began to stay in his room and only came out to eat or go to school .The only time his dad spoke to him was to shout at him and to ask him the football results on odd occasions.

When I was pregnant with my third baby, Jaxon, my fingers became so swollen I had to take off my wedding rings. I left them on the window sill in our bedroom and forgot to put them back on, then one day I went into my bedroom and I opened my wardrobe doors. I wasn't sure what I was looking for, so I closed it again.

I heard the Holy Spirit say, 'Go back to the wardrobe and look again.'

I looked again, lifting up my underwear and checking for something but not knowing what. Then I saw the box for my wedding rings.

'Oh crap, my rings. I forgot to put them back on.'

Then I began to trace my steps and realised I had left them on the window sill weeks ago. I moved the curtain and they were gone. I searched the wardrobe in a panic and then the Holy Spirit directed me to my husband's wardrobe.

I didn't usually go in his wardrobe except to hang his clothes up, but I thought maybe he had found them and put them away for me. I saw a pink slip right in front of my eyes. I knew this was no one but God because I didn't ever go through his things. I opened the pink piece of paper and saw that it was a receipt. Lindon had pawned my wedding rings without asking me or telling me. I sat on the bedroom floor in front of his wardrobe in disbelief. He pawned my wedding rings! I couldn't why because I knew how much the mortgage and council tax was he earned more than enough especially with me paying for everything else.

In September 2007 I had our third baby: a boy and by this time, life with Lindon had become unbearable, even the children were unhappy.

I was practically a single married woman. Lindon had no interest whatsoever in his children apart from Sundays, church day, where everyone could see him. He would rush to church and leave me to get the three children ready. On the odd occasion he would take the older two and leave me to bring the baby with the heavy car seat all by myself. I had really bad back pain because after having Jaxon the placenta wouldn't come out so they had to give me an epidural in my spine.

I would literally sit in church on a Sunday and watch him help carry in other women's babies in their car seats while I struggled by myself. I felt really low. This man was a fraud! He was pretending to be a totally different person in front of all these church people and none of them could see through his phony act. This man had just got done cussing me off before going to church telling me that my whole family worthless.

Oh, I forgot to mention he had banned my family from stepping foot in his house. Why? God only knows. This was the same family that welcomed him with open arms even after he had cheated on me. The same family that fed him and bought him clothes to wear when he first came from Jamaica, but now he had bought a house, we were all beneath him.

Nine months later I was driving to church and began to cry out to God. I asked him why my husband was acting this way. I couldn't understand what was going on. What happened to the nice guy I married?

I dried my eyes and walked into church. I had to sit by the door at the back because the pastor was in the middle of the opening prayer. We had to wait until she had finished and then take our seats because there was no moving around in church while someone was praying. I began to hear a woman whose face nor voice did I recognised. She began talking in tongues very loudly. I thought, *Oh crap, she is coming to me because of my conversation with God earlier.* My legs began to shake as the woman got closer and closer. I remember thinking, *Please, God, let her stop at someone else.*

I felt someone grab Jaxon out of my arms and before I knew it this woman was touching me from the top of my head to the souls of my feet. She began speaking in between tongues and English. She said God had heard my tears and he knew my heart. I instantly burst into tears. I was a wreck. I was in awe. God actually heard me.

The woman put her arms around me and hugged me. I had my face buried deep into her neck and after what seemed like five minutes or so, I felt a heavy weight across the back of my shoulders. I opened one eye in between crying and saw that the woman hugging me was about the same height and build as me, around five feet seven inches, I was confused who it was that was hugging me. It was not the arms of this slim-built woman standing in front of me. These arms were at least six feet wide. The lady went back to her seat and I was in no doubt that I had just had a supernatural encounter. I believed I was being hugged by an angel of God.

CHAPTER 9

Spiritual Jealousy?

I began to seek God deeper by reading his word daily and trying to get through life as best as I could. Lindon was still pretending on a Sunday. God was my comfort and my strength, my best friend.

A few weeks later I attended a district convention. It was actually a miracle I got there. Lindon got up, made his breakfast, got himself ready and walked straight out of the door and left me to get the three kids ready by myself. I ironed all the clothes for me and the kids, wound up the iron cord and put it back in its place behind the bedroom door. Then I heard a scream. My poor baby! Jaxon had touched the hot iron and his little fingers began to blister. I ran into the bathroom and ran them under the cold tap and started to cry. I knew the devil was trying to stop me from going to the convention, but that was not going to happen. I rocked Jaxon to sleep and got the older two ready and drove to church like a mad woman telling Satan that his tricks won't work.

I got to church on time, but my clothes were dirty and stained with baby drool and snot and my legs were dry, but at least the kids were presentable. I was sat in the middle of the church with the kids because they were the only seats left. I could see Lindon sitting right at the front of the church like some damn teacher's pet. The church was packed to capacity.

The visiting bishop began to preach and soon the church was on Holy Ghost fire. Bishop did an altar call for anyone not yet filled with the Holy Spirit to come forwards. I didn't want to leave my baby with his burnt fingers. I looked around with desperation in my eyes not knowing whether to go up or not and saw a church sister I knew from my local church. She held out her hands and took the Jaxon allowing me to go up. There were about one hundred and fifty of us at the altar and I was near the back.

I saw the bishop walking towards me. He stopped in front of me and asked me a few questions about Jesus and began to pray. It was kind of surreal how he bypassed everyone in front of me.

'I see. This was why the devil tried to stop me from coming to church today.'

I prayed and asked God to fill me with his Holy Spirit. I started to think about the way my life had suddenly changed and knew it was a spiritual attack and again asked God to fill me and told him I could not do this without him. While the bishop was praying over me, I felt something begin to stir in my belly. It was like water swirling deep in my stomach. I felt it begin to come up, then felt as though I was going to be sick but instead of throwing up, I started to speak in an unknown language. I could actually hear myself speaking in tongues. I felt weightless as though I was floating horizontally.

The bishop started to shout, 'Yes, God, yes. Thank you, Jesus.'

Everyone in the church and at the altar began to look to see who had been filled first. I saw Lindon turn around and look at me for a split second then face the altar again. Many of us were filled that day and the whole church was happy and hugging those who had received the Holy Spirit. My husband came nowhere near me.

The next time I saw him was when I arrived home. In fact, he didn't speak to me again until two weeks later.

CHAPTER 10

Church Hurt

It's 2010 we were still attending church and Lindon was still pretending except now he hardly wants to mix with the church brethren because they were also beneath him. Tasha was now nine years old and had also worked out that she should steer clear of her dad. The kids had all their birthday parties at my mum's house because my family were still too far beneath him to enter into his precious house or his presence. Lindon and I were just about on talking terms.

Sadly, a church mother had died and I heard Lindon on the phone telling another church brother that he was going to the nine night.

The next evening he got up and went. He didn't ask me if I wanted to go, he just went. I looked at the bedroom clock and he still hadn't arrived home by

10 p.m., so I decided to go to sleep. Even though things were a bit strained, I was still worried about him.

The next morning was a Saturday. I woke up at 8 a.m. and saw him awake lying on his back looking up at the bedroom ceiling.

'How was it?' I said.

He mumbled something out of his mouth.

Why was his face so upset? I knew it couldn't possibly be me. I just woke up for heaven's sake. Then he dropped the bomb that would change my whole life.

Lindon looked at me dead in the eye and accused me of telling people in the church that he was sleeping with another church sister.

What? That made no sense. Why would I tell the whole church my husband was sleeping with someone else without confronting him first?

My chest became very heavy and tight as though someone had sat on it.

'I what? Who on earth told you that? Tell me, so I can confront them.' I sat up in the bed. 'If you can't see that it's the plan from the pit of hell then I don't know what to say to you. What is going on with you?'

I picked up my mobile and called the pastor. I told her what was going down in my house and that I was going to question everyone tomorrow morning at church.

The pastor tried to calm me down and told me it was a plan from the devil and I should ignore it. She told me to come to church tomorrow and not to pay them no mind because the devil would use anyone he could. Although what she said was true, that was of no help to me at all.

How could I go to church when I wanted to kill everyone? How could church people do this? I was picturing all of their faces one by one trying to work out who started the rumour.

I didn't go to church that Sunday and by now it was all around the church and people were talking. Caroline, the woman who I supposedly said was sleeping with Lindon, called him on the Sunday evening. I asked her if she actually believed that I had said that and she said she wasn't sure. No one in that church had ever heard me speak about anyone. They didn't even have my mobile number. I only said hi and bye in church and hardly brought the conversation further, so why would she have reason to doubt me? I felt as though I was going mad. Someone somewhere had started this rumour and Lindon believed it. I think Caroline did too.

A few months went by and I kind of stopped going to church. Lindon was treating me like public enemy number one. I seriously thought I had a target on my back. I was mentally drained, but then one evening, I found the energy to go to the prayer meeting.

Were people looking or was I just being paranoid? Caroline was there. She smiled at me and tried to stretch out her arms to take Jaxon because he was her godson. Why was she smiling at me? I thought I was the one who accused her of sleeping with my husband. I gave her no eye contact and moved Jaxon over onto the other chair beside me.

The pastor said she wanted to pray for those who needed prayer. I didn't go up but the pastor called me up. She started to speak in tongues and said Satan desired to shift me as wheat but God said he was going to give me the wings of eagles and I would soar and not faint. I packed up my Bible, put the baby's coat on and left before the end. I think Caroline realised I didn't start those rumours after all, but I didn't care. I hadn't done anything to these people. Were they even aware of the amount of contention that was going on in my house? My so-called husband believed every word of the lies. I stopped going to church altogether, me and the children.

The atmosphere at home became too much. Lindon started telling the two older kids that I was a Jezebel and he told my oldest son Terry not to ask me for anything because I was nothing and no one , I had no authority.

By 2011 he was out of control. He was saying all kinds of things in front of the kids who were around fourteen, ten and four. The kids were not allowed to have friends over and Terry was not allowed to go out after school with his friends. Lindon was like a man possessed with a demonic spirit.

I couldn't take it anymore and I went to see a solicitor. I had decided to get a divorce. Once he had been served, he stopped talking to me altogether. The divorce was something I had said I never wanted to go through. The kids suffered the most and he treated them as though they belonged to someone else. In fact, he even said the two older ones were not his. We got into some really bad arguments and even though Lindon and I were living in the same house, we were living two separate lives. How could he do this to me? What had I done to deserve this, Lord?

Lindon became the king of pettiness. He would cook and make a huge mess and tell the kids to clean it up. He would scale his fish all over the freshly washed plates and leave it. When he washed his car or worked in the back garden, he would leave the doors wide open in the middle of winter and no one was allowed to close them even though we were freezing cold. He would stand at the front door and block Terry from entering when he came from school.

The kids were growing up and because of the way he was behaving, they wanted little to do with him. If I left them in the house with Lindon, they would be traumatised by the time I came home. Lindon would tell them I was no good and if they listened to me, he would beat them. He twisted Tasha's arm for not putting clothes on the radiator. I couldn't leave the kids alone with him anymore.

CHAPTER 11

Moving On

In 2013 and five court battles later, the divorce was nearly over, although I hadn't got my decree nisi yet. I was feeling so low and decided to go on this 'Facebook' I heard everyone talking about. I saw a few of my cousins and sent them friend requests, This Facebook thing was taking my mind off of all the problems at home. I noticed my cousin Jacey was friends with some guy who used to make music way back in the day.

I wondered if she knew him and wondered if we were related because we had the same last name. I called Jacey but it just so happened that she was away in Europe and her phone had broken.

I decided to inbox him and ask.

As soon as I sent that message, I instantly regretted it, but at this point I really didn't care. As far as I was concerned I wasn't married , maybe legally but it wasn't a marriage , I had checked out a long time ago. I wasn't going to church and I needed a bit of escape and to be honest, I didn't ever think I would get a reply.

About four days later I got a DM. It was him: Malcolm.

He replied back saying, 'I don't know or care if we are family, but I know what I'd like to do to you.'

What? What a damn cheek! Did he know who he was talking to? He didn't know me. He must have sent it to the wrong person. I began to look through all his pictures as his page was open. I saw loads of pictures of him with some beautiful woman.

I brushed off his crude reply and asked him if he had family in St. Catherine.

I got no reply.

Two weeks later I got another DM from Malcolm.

'I've been looking through your pictures and you are so gorgeous, you pretty coolie bitch.'

What did he say? I was looking around to see if anyone could see what this man had written to me. No one had ever called me gorgeous before. Lindon barely touched my hand, let alone called me gorgeous.

Who was this man and what was he saying to me? I knew it was wrong because I was still legally married, but the truth was I didn't care.

Malcolm said things that no one had ever said to me before.

Over the next few weeks we began talking every day via DM until one day he asked for my number.

A million things raced through my mind. *I can't give him my number. I'm still married. Why does he want my number?* From what I could gather by the comments under his pictures, he also had a wife.

After some thought, I gave him my number because it was okay to have friends. Someone to talk to. No harm done.

We began talking on the phone. I told him I was going through a divorce and, to my surprise, he told me he had been separated from his wife for two years, although he was still living there because he had no place else to go. He said his wife had caught him having an affair. At this point alarm bells should have been ringing, but just the sheer fact someone was actually listening to me rang louder.

We had a lot in common. We were both stuck in marriages with people we didn't want to be with.

He was so supportive and very understanding, not to mention charming. He was always willing to listen to me go on about my stressful divorce and the many court appearances.

I remember attending court one day and Lindon had told the judge so many lies I was shattered. I just couldn't take it anymore. I was sitting in my car parked up on some random road with tears streaming down my face. My health was suffering, I had to pay money towards legal costs, Lindon had forgotten his children even existed and, to top it off, we were still living in the same house.

I looked at my phone and it was Malcolm calling.

He knew straight away by the sound of my voice that something was wrong.

I told him I had been to court for the fourth time and that my husband was a liar and I hated him and didn't want to go home.

Malcolm suggested we meet up for a drink that very same night.

I sat up quickly and dried my tears, looked in the car mirror and thought, *Why on earth does this man want to meet up with me? He lives a glamourous lifestyle by the looks of his Facebook pictures. Why me?*

We were on the phone for about two hours and at the end he said, 'So, what do you think? We meeting up later, yeah? Meet me at the cross road for 8 p.m.'

I drove home mad with my husband but bursting with excitement inside to meet Malcolm. I remember singing to all his songs through my teens and for some strange reason, I always knew when I was younger that I was going to meet him.

I crept up the stairs, got into the shower and told my kids I was going out. I deserved it. After all, I was the one with the kids day in and day out while Lindon came and went as he pleased. He didn't even care if they had eaten or not.

I met Malcolm in a wine bar that evening. He had a shiny bald head, was quite chunky and a bit piggish-looking. He was an older man Twelve years older to be precise. with no dress sense at all. He smelt of cheap aftershave.

I said hi and he hugged me so tight I melted. I hadn't had a man near me in almost three years and it felt amazing. I felt as though I knew him because of all the time we had spent on the phone together.

We had a few drinks. Mine was a soft drink and he ordered a large glass of red wine, which he said was his favourite.

We spoke for hours. This was so new and exciting to me. He was very funny and constantly showered me with compliments. This was something I had never known before, not ever. At the end of the evening he made it clear he was interested in me.

All the way home I told myself this was wrong. We were both still married and as much as I liked him, I wasn't ready for all that again, even though I considered myself well and truly separated.

Over the next few weeks I tried to forget about Malcolm but it was really, really hard.

CHAPTER 12

New Love?

Malcolm would call me every evening even when he was at home. He would video call me, so I thought he really must be separated. Something which I found really annoying was the fact that Malcolm switched his phone off every night and didn't switch it back on until he woke up again, which was usually after 12 in the afternoon. Malcolm was a singer and didn't have a regular job.

After a few months Malcolm began to take me out. I didn't have any regrets because even though I wasn't officially divorced, it definitely wasn't a marriage and Malcolm told me his wife was also seeing two married men.

Soon after, Lindon began to get wind of Malcolm and told the court I was having an affair. They advised him he just had to face up to the fact I no longer wanted to be married to him and we just needed to sort out who was going to get what to finalise the divorce.

We went to court two further times for financial hearings which were about six months apart. Both judges said that, because I had the children, they would ask him to leave the house until our youngest was eighteen then it would be sold and divided equally. It was nearly the end of 2013 and I was finally officially divorced. Thank you, Lord.

In July 2013 we had the final financial hearing. Neither of us were represented by a barrister because it just became too expensive. I had paid thousands towards my legal aid. The judge came in and didn't even look at me except to ask me to confirm my name and take the oath. He smiled with Lindon, which I remembered thinking was a bit weird. Within fifteen minutes the judge decided he was awarding the house to Lindon. I was in shock, but I just kept thinking, *At last this is over. I am free.*

The judge said that, because I was working part time, I wouldn't be able to afford the mortgage and that the council would rehouse me because I had the kids. He said Lindon would have to pay me some money and that was it.

I didn't appeal. I just wanted all the torment to be over. I walked out of the court past Lindon who stared me in the face with the biggest grin. I caught the bus home and got there before Lindon did. I started to pack a few clothes for me and the kids and put some extra stuff into boxes. I knew that if I stayed at the house Lindon would have tormented the hell out of me, so I went to my mum's for the night and took the kids with me. Everyone I told was in disbelief. I couldn't believe that this man I had met selling drugs with nothing more than three pairs of briefs and two outfits in a suitcase had done this to me, to our kids.

The next morning I decided to go back to the house to pick up some more things. The court had given me a month to move everything out. I put my key in the lock, but it wouldn't turn. Lindon had changed the locks overnight.

I went back to my mum's house and told everyone what he had done. The two older kids were upset but hid it well. They no longer had their own rooms; we now shared a single room in a small four-bedroom house. What would I have done without my mother? She opened up her house to us and never once said no.

The kids soon settled into school and living at my mum's house, living on top of each other became the new norm.

By now Malcolm's wife had seen pictures of us on facebook and told him he had to leave, so he found a room to rent about thirty minutes away from me. He didn't own a car or work, except singing every now and again, so I helped him move all his stuff to his room in my car. Malcom and I went out all the time and everyone loved us as a couple. I usually bought all the drinks because he had no money except what he got from the government. His kids stopped speaking to him and he said it was because his wife was jealous. He said that she was an old bitch and I was young and pretty. I told him to stop calling women bitches, which he seemed to do quite a lot. He knew I didn't like that kind of talk. Even though I was no longer going to church, I still didn't like to hear swearing so he did his best to tame his mouth around me. In fact, that was the only thing I didn't like about him. Our relationship was beautiful. He was so caring and understanding and he treated me like a queen. He love bombed me right from the beginning of our relationship telling me he loved me after a month.

After about a year or so he began to speak about depression. He said it was because his kids no longer spoke to him. That must have been really hard for him. From what he told me, he was the perfect father. I would tell Malcolm about God and speak life into him to try to break the cycle.

Soon after, he began turning his phone off for days and not contacting me or opening the door when I went up to visit him, but oddly enough he would be on Facebook constantly posting pictures of himself at the gym . Then he would come back apologising, blaming the depression and declaring his undying love saying I was the only woman he had ever loved. One thing I never was was stupid. All those women he had and I was the only one he had ever loved? Yeah right!

Malcolm repeated this cycle on and off, but I stuck by him and tried to show him things would get better. Almost instantly he forced himself into the kids' lives by playing with them and wanting to take them out to the park all the time. You could say he love bombed them too. There were times when I thought he was moving a bit fast but he treated me so right, I didn't care that he didn't have any money or even a pot to piss in.

Around 2015 Malcolm asked me to marry him. He saved up £2,000 out of his gig money to buy my engagement ring. I was always a very private person, but he was big on Facebook. He didn't belch without posting about it. He asked me if I could post about him proposing to me, so I did. The post got so many likes and looking back on it now, I can see that Malcolm loved the attention.

He started to write a lot of new music and said that they were all about me.

He even called me his beautiful prize in one of them boasting and declaring his love for me.

Lindon was hopping mad that another man was around his kids. I couldn't see why as he never hardly bothered with them. I texted him to ask for our youngest son's passport which he had stolen out of my wardrobe before I moved out. He told me to take him to court if I wanted it, so that was exactly what I did.

When we went to court, a woman said she wanted to speak with the two youngest kids alone. By now Terry was over sixteen so he didn't count. When the lady from the court had finished questioning them, we went before the judge. This was the first time I had seen Lindon in a while and he was still wearing those old beat-up brown shoes I hated. The judge ruled that not only did Lindon have to give me the passport, but he would not be able to see them again until they reached eighteen years old. The kids had told the woman at the court everything Lindon had done to them. I didn't think any of us expected that.

Things were going great. I never had to see Lindon again and the kids were happy.

In 2016 Malcolm had to go to Jamacia because a relative was sick. I decided that because myself and the kids had been through so much, I was going to take them to Jamaica as well. Malcolm had already booked his ticket, so I booked my flight for the day after his also paying for two hotel rooms: one for me and Malcolm and one for the kids to share. I booked all-inclusive for two weeks in Montego Bay Jamaica.

Malcolm was his usual charming self and the kids loved him. He would joke with them a lot, which is something their dad never did.

I did begin to notice something which was slightly worrying, but those red flags kept disappearing under all the love and attention. Malcolm would drink a lot. Whilst on holiday all he wanted to do was drink all night and wake up late, then repeat the cycle. I know I didn't pay thousands of pounds to take my kids on a dream holiday to sit and wait around for him to sober up. No, sir! I booked so many excursions for us: horse riding, ziplining, climbing the falls at Dunn's River, which, of course, I paid for. It was something I wanted to do for my babies that had been through so much and deserved it. It was the holiday of a lifetime. We had an amazing time.

When we got back to England, Malcolm fell into his usual cycle of switching off his phone except now, if I disagreed with him over the slightest thing, he would block me on social media and not speak to me for weeks. I would give him time and wait for him to sort himself out. He constantly complained about not having money and seemed to be okay after me giving him some. The first thing he would buy was a big bottle of red wine. I suggested he should maybe look for a job, he didn't like that and stopped speaking to me for weeks calling me disrespectful and making him feel inferior. Also, he started to swear and call me all sorts of things by text, but never to my face.

When he came back around or needed money for something, he would unblock me and tell me he really loved me and couldn't wait to marry me. He was in the process of divorcing his ex-wife, so I put it down to stress and tried my best to help him get through it, believing we could. He was still dependant on me for money and I was buying all his clothes when he went out. I wasn't trying to buy his love; I just had a very soft heart which is something that runs in my family. This sounds really strange but I actually got used to him not speaking to me and just thought, *I will see you when I see you.*

At this point, I should have known better than to continue with the relationship, but when we were together it was genuine love, laughter and fun. It made me forget about everything I had been through with Lindon, so once more I turned a blind eye to those ever-growing red flags. Malcolm started to act funny because he wanted me to leave my mum's house and rent a house for us to live in. Was he serious right now? He wanted me to pay to rent a house for £1,600 per month just so he could live in it? I was buying him clothes, food and giving him money and, on top of it all, he wanted me to do that? We had agreed from early on that we would live separately until I got housed by the local government to save us money.

I told Malcolm that if he was unhappy we shouldn't get married, but once again he proclaimed his undying love for me and said I was the only woman he had ever loved and he couldn't imagine his life without me. Malcolm still treated me like a queen, showering me with love and being the perfect gentleman on the one hand, then falling back into depression and shutting me off. I told myself I could ignore it because, to be quite honest, he had done it so often I was used to it. I was still ignoring those big red flags that where by now slapping me all over my face.

There was a woman called Kat Bailey amongst others who started to inbox him on a regular basis and he thought it was okay as a soon-to-be married man to entertain her. He actually came clean when he realised he had forgotten to delete her message which I saw. She had been talking about me, calling me a hawk, telling him she really liked his pictures but was too scared to comment on them in case I saw. Big red flag.

CHAPTER 13

Is He Jealous of Me Too?

In 2017 I exchanged my Mercedes for a BMW and although I was still living in one room with all my kids, we made it work and we were happy. But Malcolm wasn't happy that I had bought myself a new car he kept telling me that he was jealous of me because I had it all together. The look on his face said it all and to make things worse, I bought it when he was in one of his ignoring me cycles. He thought I was making him look foolish and he wasn't happy that he didn't have a car, telling me I should get one on hire purchase for him. I laughed to myself so hard. He hinted a few more times before he realised it was never going happen. He already owed me £2,000 for two albums I paid for to be pressed. How was he in the studio making song after song without a penny to turn them into a cd's.

Red flags were coming from every direction I soon began to uncover I was the fifth woman on Facebook he had been in a relationship with, not to mention the others he'd had casual sex with. I also started to notice big inconsistencies in the stories he told about his ex-wife and children. His story changed so many times and when I brought it up to him, he got angry and agitated. I felt nasty and told him if I had any inclination in the beginning that he had slept with so many women I would not have gone anywhere near him. I was under the impression he was in a long-term committed relationship with his then wife.

He told me he had cheated throughout the whole time that they were together even sleeping with a woman called Jackie who lived opposite them. He explained it all away by saying they had been together since they were teenagers and he looked at her as a friend and even claimed the sight of her repulsed him.

I told him she was the mother of his children and he shouldn't speak about her like that. The look of contempt in his eyes… I told him everything he did would come right back to him and he needed to ask God for forgiveness. Unbeknown to me he began telling people we were having problems, which I didn't find out about until later on. A liar never likes to be caught out.

CHAPTER 14

We Got Married

In early 2018 Malcolm and I finally got married. He still wasn't working at this point, so I paid for the entire wedding by myself. I planned every aspect because although Malcolm was excited, he said it was a woman's thing and he was happy as long as it was everything I wanted.

Two weeks after getting married, we went on an amazing honeymoon to Mexico. All-inclusive for seven days which, you guessed it, I paid for. Malcolm drank alcohol all evening and slept all day. We went on two excursions which he could barely keep awake for which was hella annoying.

He was on Facebook for most of the time posting pictures of Mexico and the hotel. I noticed he wouldn't really scroll through the feed. He was obsessed with looking at his own pictures and at how many likes he got.

Whilst in Mexico, Malcolm saw a wallet he liked in the hotel shop and wanted me to buy it for him. It was £200. I said I couldn't afford it and he began to tell me about how many designer bags I had. Should I remind him that I actually worked? I decided it was best not to. His whole attitude changed and he begun to sulk, claiming he had a headache and went back to the hotel room.

After a couple of hours I joined him in the room where he was entertaining himself with Facebook. Soon the honeymoon was over and we returned to the UK.

At this point, although I was still living at my mum's, I was at Malcolm's all the time. Jaxon was eleven years old and could now go to school by himself, so I didn't have to worry about him too much and my Mum had said to me not to worry about anything she is fine with me staying at Malcolm's. So I went to work from Malcolm's, went home, checked on Jaxon and the older two and back to Malcolm's, which also gave the kids a bit more space in the bedroom. I was extremely tired at this point because I was leaving Malcolm's at 6 a.m. Then, when I returned to Malcolm's in the evening, he had only just woken up a few hours earlier so wanted me to stay up all night with him until he fell asleep at 4 or 5 in the morning. I was burning the candle at both ends to try to please him and when I could no longer stay awake, he would call me boring and try to make me feel guilty for going to sleep. He would start to say things like I might as well go home and that there was no point in me staying with him. Was this man for real?

While he was getting all the sleep he needed during the day and looking amazing, I was looking haggard being deprived of sleep all the time. I was finding it hard to concentrate. After a few weeks Malcolm began to complain about how much he wanted the wallet in Mexico and said he felt like shit because he couldn't afford it. Reluctantly, I bought up the subject of him trying to get a job again. Who told me to say that?

One day, whilst at work, Malcolm text me to tell me not to bother coming round and that he wanted to be by himself. Huh? Okay, I knew he did this crap before but we had just had a beautiful wedding and not to mention just come back from a five-star honeymoon to Mexico.

As soon as I finished work, I tried to call him. It went straight to voicemail. I saw he was on Facebook, so I messaged him. I waited, but after a couple of hours there was still no reply. Towards the end of the evening, the kids started to ask me what I was doing back home and told me to go back to Malcolm's. I decided that, although I was tired, I was going to drive to his house.

I rang the doorbell. Edmond who lived in one of the other rooms answered the door.

'Hi, Edmond. Is Malcolm in? I've been trying to call him, but can't get through.'

Edmond said, 'Sorry. Malcolm doesn't want to speak to you. I can't let you in.'

Wait? Sorry? Excuse me? I had only been married for just over a month and he didn't want to see me? I got back into my car in sheer disbelief. I went back onto Facebook to see if he was online to find out he had blocked me; I couldn't see his page at all. I drove back to my mum's house in a daze. I couldn't believe this big fifty-nine-year-old man was behaving this way. This cut way deeper than before. I kept having flashbacks to our wedding day a month earlier and how happy we were. What had I done to this man, God? All I ever tried to do was look after him. How could this man, who called me his everything only a week ago, cut me off like this?

I drove back to my mum's feeling like a fool. What would I tell everyone? What would I tell the kids?

Malcolm ignored me for five whole months. No texts, no phone calls, nothing. I would see people who we knew on the street and they would ask me how my husband was. At this point they knew more about how he was doing than me. At least they could see his

Facebook posts. I began thinking, *What if something happened to me or the kids?* I could actually die and he would have been none the wiser. Then it hit me like a ton of bricks. I had jumped out of the frying pan and into the fire.

CHAPTER 15

He Unblocked Me

It was now the end of August 2018 and my birthday was in two days. I heard my phone vibrate five times. It was Malcolm. After five months, he had finally unblocked me.

I picked up my phone and began to read all five messages he had sent. He started his sentence with an explosion of obscenities towards me, telling me everything was my fault and the reason he blocked me was because I was so belligerent and I was every sort of female dog under the sun. He told me I was worthless and he didn't want to be married to me anymore and I had wasted his life!

My first reaction was to laugh. Did he send this to the wrong person? Surely this wasn't for me. He told me his dad had died in Jamaica while we were apart and it was all my fault. He told me he had to borrow money to pay for his flight to go to the funeral and he couldn't mourn properly because of all the stress I had put him through. And the final sentence?

'I hate your guts, bitch, and I want a divorce. This marriage is nothing but a sham.'

I thought long and hard before replying. Now I knew I didn't do anything to this man, but I was conscious of the fact he mentioned his dad died. I felt really bad because I had spoken to his dad by video about 6 months before and his dad had asked me to look after him.

After a few hours of reading and digesting his messages, I thought long and hard about my reply so I wouldn't cause him any more stress on top of what he was already going through. I couldn't reply as he had blocked my phone number. This time he had unblocked me on Facebook, but he had also unfriended me. I could see the pictures he was posting, but I couldn't message him.

I tossed and turned all that night, for most nights really. It was a combination of the menopause, Malcolm's behaviour and all the abusive text messages he had sent to me. Was this really the behaviour of a fifty-eight-year-old man?

I checked WhatsApp again to reread the messages he had sent me from earlier and saw he was typing a message. More vile abuse. I mean, what else did I expect from him? Did I expect him to confess his undying love for me like he did before we were married?

I fell asleep still confused and bewildered by his very strange behaviour. I woke up to yet another long text telling me he was giving me a chance to apologise for what I did and that I should go to his house at 7pm that evening. I read it in disbelief. What should I apologise for?

At 7 p.m. I rang the bell. He had a half smile and asked if I brought wine with me. I said no and he asked if I could get him a bottle, so I went to the shop and brought the wine. He drank a few large glasses, not saying much at all. I noticed he had a couple of bottles of spirits that were almost finished.

About 2 a.m., after many glasses of wine, Malcolm began to tell me he really loved me, but I kept putting him through hell. I had a whole conversation in my head thinking, *Now I know you're mad.*

He stopped short of blaming me for his dad's death. He suggested we should go out at the weekend as it was a bank holiday and my birthday. I ordered the tickets to get into the club and we went out. The conversation flowed a bit better, but he was still acting weird. He didn't show me any affection at all. It was as though I should have been grateful for him taking me out with my money.

CHAPTER 16

Malcolm Has a Job

In February 2019 Malcolm got a job. I was so happy for him even though it was night work. Maybe now he could treat me for a change. Hopefully things would get better now.

Within two months of Malcolm starting work, he bought a car on hire purchase. He had bad credit because he had taken out £25,000 on a credit card to go to Egypt when he was with his ex-wife and decided not to pay it back, so his monthly payments were quite high. He asked me to 'lend' him the money to pay for his car insurance, but I said I couldn't afford it. Then lockdown happened.

I continued to work all through the pandemic because I was an essential key worker. I bought masks, hand sanitiser and loads of food for Malcolm to make sure he was okay. He was working nights and I was working days. Now we saw each other less and less.

Malcolm decided it wasn't working between us and he didn't want to be married anymore. He blocked me once again. I didn't see Malcolm much over the next few months, so I just got on with life. He briefly unblocked me on WhatsApp to tell me a woman my sister Helen had lived next door to over ten years ago told him I used to be a prostitute.

I was angry, so angry. I sent him a voice note laughing it off.

'Yeah, that's right,' I said, 'And you owe me loads of money for my services.'

At this point any love that I had for him was disappearing. I really didn't care what he said or believed anymore. I had had enough of his shit. I told him not to call my phone ever again. He sent me back a voice note stating he knew the woman was lying and that I should fight her. This big grey back, useless excuse of a man really thought I was stupid, didn't he?

After a few months Malcolm called me out of the blue and said he needed to go to Jamaica to sort some things out. He said he really loved his dad and was cut up over his death, Again I tried to console him and told him I was there for him if he needed me. He asked me if I would go to Jamaica with him in October.

I agreed and booked my flight for the week after his because his flight was full. We agreed he would sort his business out and meet me at the airport on the day of my arrival. Then we would both get on the coach to the hotel in Ochio Rios and spend the final six days together. Everything was good.

I helped Malcolm pack his suitcase and off he went. Two days after leaving it was Malcolm's 59th birthday and he put up a big post on Facebook. He had hundreds of women sending him birthday messages and I also noticed that two women he'd had casual sex with before he met me had also sent messages, which he put a love heart on. Something stirred inside of me and I thought, *Why does this man still interact so faithfully with the women he used to sleep with?*

I was upset because, according to Malcolm, everything about one particular women was gross including her lady parts. He said he wasn't interested in her, but she wouldn't leave him alone. I found it totally disrespectful and told him when he called me. I asked him why he needed to interact with these two in particular, to which he replied I was being stupid and insecure.

I told him I was going to DM the one called Dione who he said wouldn't leave him alone because according to her he was 'the one'. I would tell her to stop messaging him. He said he didn't care, so I did it.

I messaged her and told her she should stop messaging Malcolm and asked her why she still felt the need to text him considering she had her own man. I told her that while Malcolm was sleeping with her, he was also sleeping with two others at the same time which was what Malcolm said out of his own mouth. Dione sent my message to Malcolm.

He called me telling me to grow up and accused me of being an immature little girl. He accused me of being overbearing and said he couldn't stand me and hung up the phone. I tried to call back, but couldn't get through.

The next week I got on the plane as planned and landed late at night at Montego Bay. I waited for Malcolm until nearly everyone had left the airport. I decided to get on a coach to the hotel. I checked in and fell asleep as I was shattered. I messaged Malcolm the next morning, but got no reply that day or the day after.

Finally, on the third day, I got a DM from Malcolm. He asked me if I knew how much trouble I had caused and called me all sorts of nasty things. He said I had no right to message Dione. Why did I find it so difficult to believe my husband was putting another woman's feelings before mine? I wasn't sure how much more I could take. This man had no consideration for me at all.

I went back to the UK and didn't hear from Malcolm until October 2020, a week before his sixtieth birthday, to be precise. I was just getting on with life. In fact, I was enjoying it. I missed Malcolm, but I always told myself that I came into this world by myself and I would leave by myself. I prayed a lot for Malcolm especially after finding out he had spent two weeks in a mental health unit after suffering a breakdown before we met.

Things started to make more and more sense and I realised it was nothing I had done. This had been going on for over twenty years. I mentioned to the kids that it was Malcolm's sixtieth birthday soon.

Jaxon, who was twelve at the time, said, 'I bet he calls you to go out.'

You guessed it, within hours of Jaxon saying it Malcolm had called me to tell me he had realised how much he loved me and he couldn't be without me anymore. This went right over my head and his flattery was actually boring me now because I realised he didn't know how to tell the truth .

Jaxon looked at me and we laughed. The kids were completely fed up with him by now and, to tell you the truth, if we weren't married to him I wouldn't have entertained him. I knew he was using me but I took him out to a local wine bar anyway, bought a cake and had a massive '60' balloon waiting at the table before we arrived. We were still in lockdown at that point, so there weren't many places open or many people allowed at a venue at one time. I sang happy birthday and we had a nice time. I videoed him which he put on Facebook later that night, but cut me out of the video. I began to go through all his pictures and saw he deleted almost all of the pictures he had of me, including our wedding day.

I went back to my mum's the next day. I wasn't even excited to be with him and I realised the love I had for him was practically gone. I was going off him, my eyes no longer lit up when I saw him. With him working at night and me during the day, it was hard to spend any real time together. He wouldn't be disturbed when he was sleeping during the day, but wanted me to stay awake with him at night. I decided I wasn't going to do that anymore, I decided to put me first. I didn't see him again until two weeks after but in between that time he had asked me to lend him money for his car insurance, again I told him I couldn't afford it. In all the years that we had been together he hardly ever put his hand in his pocket always borrowing money from people, what a turn off!

When I arrived at his house, he looked at me and said, 'Why have you come here?'

I thought, *Here we go again. Mad man in full effect.*

He asked me to leave and said he wanted a divorce. He asked me for his front door keys back which he had only just given me a few weeks ago. What a joker.

I told him he would have to pay for the divorce because he paid nothing towards the wedding or honeymoon. I picked up my belongings and left.

In January 2021 he began to harass me via email to hurry up and divorce him. I thought he may have a woman, although he didn't confirm it at the time. I decided to drag my feet before signing it and he began to tell me all kinds of rubbish. I asked him to stop being rude because I had never been rude to him, but he got even more vile and then changed his WhatsApp picture to his new woman. He said I was worthless and I that lived in one room.

I started to laugh because he was also renting one room in a stranger's house. At least I was living with my mum. I sent him a voice note laughing because his new woman was older than me by about ten years, even though he had always said he didn't want no old dried-up bitch. She also wore a weave which was funny to me because he would laugh at all the women's wigs when we would go out saying they looked as though they had a cat on their head. At that point I blocked him before he could reply to me.

I signed the divorce papers and we were divorced by July 2022. I felt as free as a bird. It was weird really because I was unusually happy and the peace I had came from no one but God. The next few months I did nothing but work while he posted millions of pictures of his new victim, I mean wife-to-be, on Facebook so I was told. Many friends who knew us a couple said he was disgraceful and they could no longer stand him, but they knew what he was like because he spoke about anyone and everyone all the time even his so-called good friends in the music industry.

CHAPTER 17

When God Closes a Door, He Always Opens a New One

I did nothing but work and watch T. D. Jakes, an American preacher. His messages were so powerful and encouraging. I was drawing closer to God.

The week after the divorce was final, my sister Kerry asked me to go with her to the same church I had been filled with the Holy Spirit all those years ago. They were having some kind of mid-week evening meeting. I walked in and felt at home instantly. Within twenty minutes of praying I began to speak in tongues again. I was overwhelmed with the love of God.

The following week, the bishop asked if anyone needed prayer at the end of the service. I didn't move but he told his daughter, who I just so happened to be sitting next to, to ask me to go up. I went to the altar and someone began to pray for me. She told me things that no one could ever have known and she said that God had his eye on me. She said God was going to completely change my life and that Egyptian I once saw, I would never see again. (Exodus 14:13) meaning that I would never go through that again .

I went back to my mum's and told my family. Whilst telling them, God brought to my remembrance what my pastor had spoken over me ten years earlier about God giving me wings of eagles. I was dumbstruck because, to be honest, I had totally forgotten about it.

In August 2022 I was offered a place to live by the local council. I was so happy my life was finally moving forwards. Over the next few months, God began to drop things into my spirit. He said he had closed the door because where he was taking me Malcolm could not go. I began to realise that as much as I was praying for my marriage it was not the will of God for my life. God told me to let go of unforgiveness and that he would prepare a table for me in the presence of my enemies. I didn't need to get revenge on Malcolm or hold up any hate in my heart for him.

I am the happiest I have ever been in my entire adult life. God has quickened my spirit and healed my heart. I look forward to the next chapter of my life with God. When I look back through my life and see he was always there.

God never left me.

'Remember ye not the former things, neither consider the things of old. Behold, I will do a new thing; now it shall spring forth; shall ye not know it? I will even make a way in the wilderness, And rivers in the desert.' (Isiah 43:18–19)